Salter Dual Air Fryer Cookbook for Beginners UK

365-Day Delicious & Healthy Recipes with British Measurements & Ingredients to Help You Create Gourmet Meals for Family and Friends.

Tanacy Beaker

© Copyright 2022 Tanacy Beaker - All Rights Reserved.

In no way is it legal to reproduce, duplicate, or transmit any part of this document by either electronic means or in printed format. Recording of this publication is strictly prohibited, and any storage of this material is not allowed unless with written permission from the publisher. All rights reserved.

The information provided herein is stated to be truthful and consistent, in that any liability, regarding inattention or otherwise, by any usage or abuse of any policies, processes, or directions contained within is the solitary and complete responsibility of the recipient reader. Under no circumstances will any legal liability or blame be held against the publisher for any reparation, damages, or monetary loss due to the information herein, either directly or indirectly.

Respective authors own all copyrights not held by the publisher.

Legal Notice:

This book is copyright protected. This is only for personal use. You cannot amend, distribute, sell, use, quote or paraphrase any part of the content within this book without the consent of the author or copyright owner. Legal action will be pursued if this is breached.

Disclaimer Notice:

Please note the information contained within this document is for educational and entertainment purposes only. Every attempt has been made to provide accurate, up-to-date and reliable, complete information. No warranties of any kind are expressed or implied. Readers acknowledge that the author is not engaging in the rendering of legal, financial, medical or professional advice.

By reading this document, the reader agrees that under no circumstances are we responsible for any losses, direct or indirect, which are incurred as a result of the use of information contained within this document, including, but not limited to, errors, omissions, or inaccuracies.

Table of Contents

Introduction 5

Chapter 1: Breakfast 17

Chapter 2: Vegetables 26

Chapter 3: Poultry 31

Chapter 4: Meats 39

Chapter 5: Casseroles, Frittatas, and Quiches 47

Chapter 6: Appetizers and Snacks 56

Chapter 7: Desserts 65

Conclusion 71

Appendix recipe Index 72

INTRODUCTION

This amazing Salter Dual Cook Pro Air Fryer allows you to quickly and easily fry, grill, and roast your favourite meals while using little to no oil. This twin-independent fryer has a 60-minute timer, adjustable temperature control, and pause and restart cooking features.

It can cook a wide range of dishes, making it perfect for making homemade chips or wedges, pork, spring rolls, filled veggies, and quiche. This air fryer includes 12 cooking options and a chic sensor touch control LED display, making it perfect for any family dinner. The fryer has a 1600 W power rating, a 200°C maximum temperature range, and two 3.7L frying racks for independent dual cooking.

Even though it's only been a week, I've already cooked everything from fries and nuggets to a complete roast on a tray. The first aspect of the baskets that I appreciate is their shape; rectangular spaces are much more useful than round ones in terms of both the amount of usable space and the ability to use a greaseproof or baking paper. Although the dual capacity aids in keeping various items apart, prepare them separately, such as when preparing fries and nuggets, as doing so may cause the covered fries to become a little soggy. It is easy and intuitive to use the Sync and Match settings.

- When compared to the energy required to cook a chicken in a 1.8 kW electric oven, using this dual air fryer can help you save 64% on energy costs.
- Thanks to the temperature adjustment and 60-minute timer, you have control over each compartment, which enables you to cook several items simultaneously.
- With a temperature pause and resume feature, the sync and match cook functions enable both compartments to be ready at the same time.
- This Dual Air fryer offers a healthier option for deep-frying while maintaining the same fantastic taste for the entire family.

- For preparing a range of meat, fish, and vegetables as well as bread and cakes, a cooking chart and several recipes are provided.
- This 7.4L fryer includes two separate 3.7L frying trays with a twin basket design, making it perfect for cooking several dishes or larger quantities.
- You have control over each compartment thanks to the temperature adjustment and 60-minute timer, which enables you to cook several items simultaneously.
- With a temperature pause and resume feature, the sync and match cook functions enable both compartments to be ready at the same time.
- This Dual Air fryer offers a healthier option to deep-frying while maintaining the same fantastic taste for the entire family.
- For preparing a range of meat, fish, and vegetables as well as bread and cakes, a cooking chart and a number of recipes are provided.

Standard air fryers are a terrific method to prepare healthier roasted or fried food with less oil, but you can usually only fit one recipe in them. You'll have to prepare one of them somewhere if you want fries and sausages or chicken breast with corn on the cob. Dual air fryers like the Salter Dual Air fill that need. You can perfectly prepare two distinct items with two separate baskets that operate independently of one another.

Design and components

- Large yet not overly ugly
- Large touch panel control, but with a frightening maximum temperature of 200°C.

In essence, the Salter Dual Air combines two air fryers side by side. You can use one side independently of the other to cook one meal or two dishes, each with the option of having a different set of settings if necessary. The Ninja Foodi Dual Zone, which is presently our favorite all-around air fryer, has a similar configuration, so that's a good place to start.

Each of the two 3.7-liter non-stick baskets in the Salter Dual Air includes a removable food tray. There is a catch, though. You can't fit a single huge item across both parts, giving it a generous 7.4 liters of cooking space. You won't be able to fit larger objects, such as a small chicken, in the two zones between them, despite the fact that they can cook a tremendous amount of food.

There is one more restriction that applies only to a particular fryer. The Dual Air's temperature maximum is 200°C, whereas the Ninja Foodi Dual Zone's Max Crisp mode reaches 240°C. That's plenty for many foods, but as my experiments showed, it's not quite enough to get the greatest browning on things like chips and other things that require intense searing or crisping.

The two baskets of this air fryer have a dual-skinned front that keeps things pretty cool while in operation, but neither the baskets nor their food trays are dishwasher safe, while I'm complaining. That might be a hassle if you're as lazy about washing dishes as I am. Finally, there is no shake reminder, which is important to ensure that meals brown evenly.

The Salter Dual Air is very similar to using any other air fryer, with the added complexity of having to create programs for each basket. It provides a number of pre-programmed modes for different food varieties, just like many other air fryers. I generally found it easier to use the manual mode to adjust the temperature and time I needed, even if these may be beneficial once you understand how to use them.

Similar to the Ninja Foodi Dual Zone, the Dual Air gives users the option of controlling their two baskets jointly or separately. By default, you can set a temperature and a start time for each, and both will operate simultaneously. In Sync mode, the longer program begins before the shorter one does, allowing both to finish cooking at the same time. Last but not least, the Match Cook mode allows you to cook multiple of the same dish with the same settings on both sides.

Prior to First Use

STEP 1: Wipe the air fryer main unit with a soft, wet cloth and dry it completely before connecting the air fryer to the main power source.

STEP 2: Wash the cooking trays with a non-stick coating and the cooking compartments in warm, soapy water, then thoroughly rinse and dry.

STEP 3: Set the main unit of the air fryer at a user-comfortable height on a firm, heat-resistant surface.

NOTE: A faint smoke or odour may be released while using the air fryer for the first time. This is typical and will pass quickly. During use, make sure there is enough ventilation around the air fryer. It is recommended to run the air fryer for around 10 minutes without any food before using it for the first time. This will stop any initial smoke or odor from detracting from the flavor of the meal.

Construction of the Dual Air

STEP 1: Insert the cooking trays with the non-stick coating into the cooking sections, making sure they are positioned firmly.

STEP 2 : is to insert the cooking compartments into the air fryer's main unit while ensuring that the display numbers and cooking compartment numbers correspond.

NOTE: The air fryer is sent pre-built. Before use, the cooking compartments must be tightly closed; otherwise, the air fryer won't function.

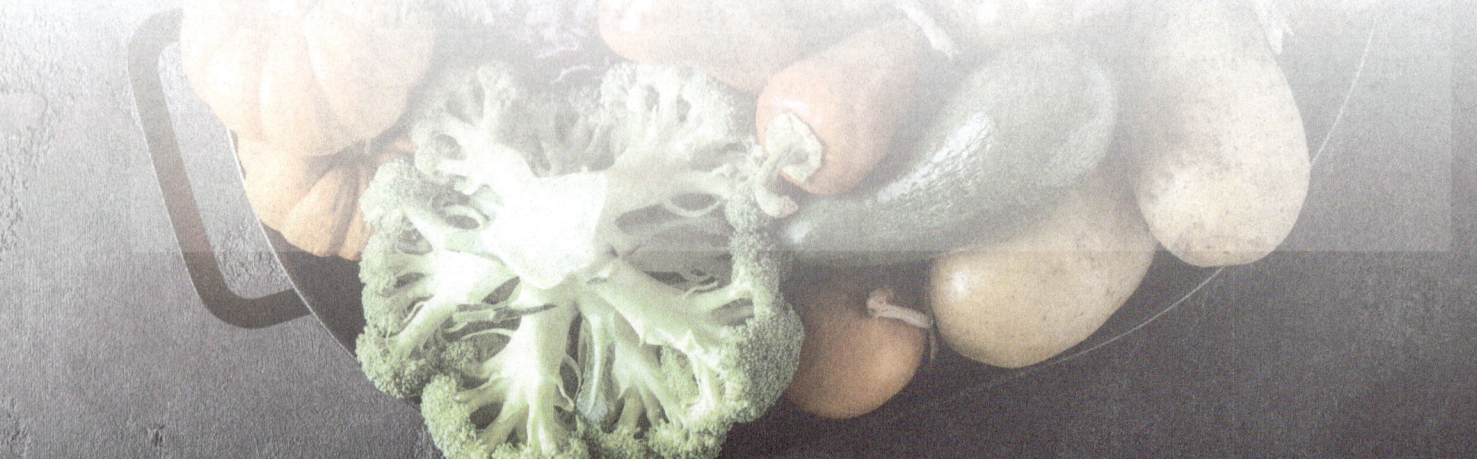

How to use the Control Panel

The item will beep and the power button will light up to show that it is powered when the air fryer is plugged in and turned on at the main power source. For the air fryer to turn on, press the power button.

Automatic Setting

The food that is cooked affects the time and temperature settings, which can be manually adjusted. The LED display will start to show lines when the air fryer is prepared for programming. Toggle between "1" and "2" to select the appropriate compartment. Press the manual button, then the time control buttons to vary the cooking time, up to a maximum of 60 minutes, to adjust the setting manually (or up to a max. of 24 hours for dehydration). To change the cooking temperature, tap the temperature control buttons. The range is 50 to 200 °C (or a maximum of 60 °C for dehydration). Make no changes to the other compartment if you're only using one. To start cooking, press the start/pause button.

NOTE: For more details and cooking instructions, consult the recipe booklet.

Preset Activities

The function buttons can also be used to set time and temperature settings; when pressed, they alternate between time and temperature presets for cooking different dishes. The time and temperature control buttons can then be used to change these presets as needed.

Holding down the time and temperature control buttons will allow you to make fast adjustments to the time and temperature.

Press the start/pause button to start heating after the temperature and time have been chosen. During use, the time and temperature can be adjusted.

The air fryer will turn off and the timer will beep when the food has finished frying and the predetermined amount of time has passed.

By tapping the drawer number and using the time and temperature control buttons, the time and temperature can be changed at any time while cooking.

Cooking will pause if the cooking chamber is removed during the process; re-insert the cooking compartment to continue.

Press and hold the power button to turn the air fryer off.

Utilizing Sync Setting the Cook

Use the "sync" setting when cooking various dishes at various times and temperatures in each compartment to ensure that both cook at the same time.

STEP 1: Press the sync cook button in the first step, and it will light up to indicate that the desired setting has been chosen.

STEP 2: Tap "1" and, using the guidelines in the "Using the Control Panel" section, make the necessary adjustments for the first cooking compartment.

STEP 3: Tap "2" to repeat for the second cooking chamber.

STEP 4: To start cooking, press the start/pause button.

How to Use the Match Cook Setting?

When cooking the same dishes in both cooking compartments, use the match option to ensure that both cooking compartments are finished at the same time.

STEP 1: Press the match cook button to pick the setting. The match cook button will light.

STEP 2: Following the directions in the section under "Using the Control Panel," in STEP 2 adjust the necessary settings for both cooking compartments.

STEP 3: To start cooking, press the start/pause button.

NOTE: While the device is plugged in, the power button will remain lighted.

By means of the Dual Air

STEP 1: Connect the air fryer to the mains power source and turn it on. The air fryer will beep and the power button will light up to show that the appliance is plugged in.

Step 2: Press the power button to turn on the air fryer. When the air fryer is ready for programming, lines will appear on the LED display.

STEP 3: Comply with the directions in the "Using the Control Panel" section. To change the time or temperature as needed, press the buttons for the time and temperature controls.

STEP 4: After the frying compartment(s) have heated, remove them from the air fryer by yanking on the handle. Place the cooking compartment(s) on a surface that is stable, flat, and heat-resistant.

STEP 5: Add the ingredients to the nonstick cooking tray, slide the cooking compartment(s) back into the air fryer main unit to close it, and then repeat with the remaining cooking compartment(s).

STEP 6: Adjust the cooking time and temperature using the digital control panel according to the needs of the ingredients. The function buttons can also be used to set time and temperature settings; when pressed, they alternate between time and temperature presets for cooking different dishes. The time and temperature control buttons can then be used to change these presets as needed.

STEP 7: It might be necessary to shake some components midway through the cooking process. Using the cooking compartment handle, remove the cooking

compartment(s) from the air fryer main unit. Slide back into the air fryer main unit after giving the cooking compartment(s) a little shake to resume cooking.

STEP 8: The air fryer will beep repeatedly and turn off once cooking is finished and the designated amount of time has passed. Verify if the ingredients are prepared; if not, close the cooking compartment(s) and put the contents back into the air fryer's main unit. To adjust the cooking time appropriately, use the digital control panel. Empty the food's contents into a bowl or a plate if it has been cooked. Using heat-resistant tongs is recommended if the meal is bulky or delicate.

NOTE: Before beginning to cook, make sure the air fryer is hot. Use the time and temperature control buttons as necessary to adjust the cooking time or temperature setting while it is being used. The settings on the air fryer will be changed automatically. 30 minutes or so should pass before touching or cleaning the air fryer.

AVOID: Avoid pouring the food directly onto a plate or bowl since excess oil may pool at the bottom of the cooking compartment(s) and leak onto the food or serving bowl. When using the cooking compartment(s), use caution when opening and shutting them because they will get quite hot.

WARNING: Even when the air fryer is turned off, nominal voltage is still present. Turn off and unplug the air fryer from the main power source to turn it off permanently.

Performance

- A higher maximum temperature would be preferable.
- Not too loud, save for the key's beeps.

This fryer may be used to cook a variety of items with respectable results. I first cooked Quorn nuggets and frozen chips with it. The latter was ideal, but the former, although having 20 minutes at the highest temperature of 200°C, could have used additional crisping. I cooked subsequent batches a little bit longer because I couldn't raise the temperature and got better results.

When roasting some new potatoes to make shabby handmade wedges, the Dual Air did a fantastic job. My kids enjoyed the outcome when I just chopped them in half, coated them in olive oil, and cooked them at maximum power for 18 minutes.

Other dishes were less noteworthy. For instance, I was unable to get frozen hash browns to crisp up quite as much as I desired. Although the Proscenia T22 only reaches 5°C hotter than the regulated top temperature, I still received flawless results from it. Even though the corn on the cob was just fine, it wasn't evenly roasted or as wonderfully caramelized as it might be on a grill. Even so, it performed a good job at cooking frozen Quorn sausages.

You're probably going to use the Dual Air's sync mode a lot when cooking a meal, much like I discovered with the Ninja Foodi Dual Zone. Dialing up two different programs and then turning on the Dual Air to have everything delivered ready at once is incredibly beneficial. However, this fryer provides extra flexibility for those occasions when you need it. Practically speaking, you can program each side separately from the other. For instance, you may bake on tray two for 40 minutes while preparing a variety of different dishes in tray one.

The Dual Air used a max of 1,708 watts throughout my tests, which is significantly less than you'd anticipate from a regular oven while having two strong components. Additionally, air fryers save time by using the heating element less because they warm up faster than an oven. In spite of this, Dual Air consumed 0.55 kWh while preparing the chip and nugget lunch. If you pay 30p per kWh, that comes to about 16p.

Even though this air fryer makes fan noise, all air fryers do. I recorded 47.6 dB at a distance of 15 cm, which decreased to 40.7 dB at a distance of 1 m and is easily drowned out in a busy kitchen. Less appealing to me were its constant key beeps, which are just as loud as the alert when food is ready and cannot be turned off. The Dual Air would definitely ruin your morning fry-up surprise if you were looking to impress someone.

Rules of Conduct

- Before using, make sure the cooking sections are properly installed. The air fryer won't operate if you don't do it.
- Cooking containers should only be held by their handle.
- When removing the cooking containers, exercise caution since steam may release.

Don't:

- The non-stick-coated cooking trays should not be removed before inverting the cooking sections since this could cause extra oil that has accumulated at the bottom of the cooking compartments to spill out onto the plate.
- Covering the air fryer or its air inlets will interfere with the airflow and may influence the way food cooks.
- Oil or another liquid should be added to the cooking chambers. Do not touch the cooking sections while using them or immediately afterward since they become very hot. Instead, only hold each cooking compartment by its handle.

Maintenance and Care

Switch off the air fryer and unhook it from the main power source before beginning any cleaning or maintenance, and then wait until it has completely cooled.

STEP 1: Use a soft, damp towel to wipe the main unit of the air fryer, then completely dry it.

STEP 2: Wash the cooking trays with a non-stick coating and the cooking compartments in warm, soapy water, then thoroughly rinse and dry.

Avoid submerging the main unit of the air fryer in water or any other liquid.

Never clean the air fryer or its accessories with abrasive or harsh cleaning products or scorers as this could result in damage.

NOTE: After every usage, the air fryer needs to be cleaned.

Was it simple to use?

The touch-sensitive panel was quite intuitive and signaled the 12 preset settings of the air fryer with little icons. Both the time and the temperature may be changed, allowing you to a play if you want to. You can use the cooking function guide included in the instruction handbook as a starting point for temperatures and cooking times, however, the directions for cooking vegetables were rather ambiguous.

Separate from this are the choices for "sync cook," where you specify the temperatures and cooking times for various meals in each drawer so they will all be done at the same time. The match-cook setting prevents you from having to preset the drawers twice if you're cooking in double portions. Or, single travelers have the choice to manually cook.

The air fryer preheated automatically once we choose the function, and it beeped to let us know when to add ingredients.

Frequently Asked Questions

Can you use a Salter dual air fryer to cook an entire chicken?

You can cook the chicken in the air fryer without adding any oil or seasonings, and it will cook and taste just fine. However, if you want the skin of the chicken to be particularly crispy, I suggest doing so.

Is oil necessary for a Salter air fryer?

Yes, and for roughly 75% of what you prepare, you should use oil in some manner. Knowing that you can use an air fryer to avoid having to deep-fry meals and then learning that it requires oil to cook can be misleading.

Does my air fryer need to be unplugged every time I use it?

Avoid Leaving It Plugged In

Like a Crock-Pot, an air fryer should never be left plugged in. Always unplug an air fryer in case you forget to turn it off.

Chapter 1: Breakfast

Air Fryer Tilapia Recipe

Prep Time: 5 Mins
Cook Time: 8 Mins   Serves: 2

Ingredients:

- 2 fillets Tilapia
- 1 teaspoon Paprika optional
- ¼ teaspoon Garlic powder
- ¼ teaspoon Onion granules
- ¼ teaspoon Black pepper
- ½ teaspoon Parsley
- Salt to taste
- 1 tablespoon Olive oil

Directions:

1. In a bowl, mix the salt, black pepper, garlic powder, onion granules, parsley, and paprika together.
2. Brush the fish with olive oil and sprinkle the seasoning on it.
3. Put the fish fillets in the air fryer, brush the top with olive oil, and sprinkle the seasoning all over the top as well.
4. Brush with olive oil.
5. Set air fryer to 180°C and air fry tilapia for 8-10 minutes or until cooked through and flaky.
6. No need to flip tilapia during cooking.
7. Remove carefully from the air fryer using a spatula.
8. The spatula will help lift the fish fillet off the air fryer basket without breaking up.

Nutritional Value (Amount per Serving):

Calories: 130; Fat: 2.17; Carb: 4.28; Protein: 23.9

Air Fried Boiled Eggs

Prep Time: 5 Mins
Cook Time: 12 Mins   Serves: 6

Ingredients:

- 6 eggs

Directions:

1. Set temperature to 150°C and set time to 12 minutes. Press START/STOP to begin

preheating.
2. When the unit beeps to signify it has preheated, place eggs onto the air fryer tray. Press the START/STOP to begin cooking. If you prefer soft boiled eggs, remove at 8 minutes, if you prefer hard boiled cook for 12 minutes.
3. Serve hot with toast or cold with a salad.

Nutritional Value (Amount per Serving):

Calories: 130; Fat: 9.64; Carb: 1.02; Protein: 8.97

Boiled Eggs With Crispy Asparagus And Parma Ham Soldiers

Prep Time: 5 Mins
Cook Time: 10 Mins   Serves: 4

Ingredients:

- 8 asparagus spears
- 4 slices parma ham
- Seasoning
- Vegetable oil spray
- 4 eggs

Directions:

1. Bring a saucepan of water to the boil. Wash and trim the ends from the asparagus and cook in the boiling water for 2-3 minutes. Drain then rinse under cold running water to cool.
2. Cut each slice of Parma ham in half and wrap a slice around each piece of asparagus, season and spray lightly with oil then lay on the air fryer tray.
3. Set the air fryer temperature to 200°C and cook the asparagus for 8 minutes until the ham is crisp.
4. Meanwhile, bring a small pan of water to the boil, gently submerge the eggs into the water and set a timer for 4 minutes for dippy eggs. Remove from the pan, place in an egg cup and serve with the crispy asparagus and Parma ham soldiers.

Nutritional Value (Amount per Serving):

Calories: 165; Fat: 11.55; Carb: 1.65; Protein: 13.02

Tuna Pasta Melt

Prep Time: 15 Mins
Cook Time: 25 Mins   Serves: 4

Ingredients:

- 150g half fat crème fraîche
- 180g light fat soft cheese
- 2 tbsp cornflour, mixed with
- 2 tbsp cold water
- 1 tbsp dijon mustard
- 400ml hot vegetable stock
- 300g wholewheat penne
- pasta, cooked as directed
- on the pack
- 2 x 145g cans tuna chunks
- in spring water, drained
- 200g can sweetcorn,
- drained
- 140g frozen peas, defrosted
- 50g half fat cheddar
- cheese, grated
- Salt and black pepper
- 1 tbsp chopped parsley

Directions:

1. To prepare the sauce, put the crème fraîche, soft cheese, cornflour and mustard in a bowl and whisk to combine. Stir in the hot stock, and season with a pinch of salt and black pepper.
2. Put the cooked pasta, tuna, sweetcorn, peas and grated cheese into a 24cm x 5cm deep square roasting dish. Pour the sauce over the pasta and stir gently to coat everything in the sauce.
3. Place the roasting tin on the cooking tray of the air fryer and set the temperature to 180°C for 25 minutes. Give the pasta melt a stir halfway through cooking.
4. Serve in warm bowls and sprinkle the parsley over the tuna
5. pasta melt.

Nutritional Value (Amount per Serving):

Calories: 1142; Fat: 105.1; Carb: 36.55; Protein: 23.62

Smoked Salmon, Scrambled Egg And Avocado Toast

Prep Time: 5 Mins
Cook Time: 10 Mins   Serves: 4

Ingredients:

- 2 ripe avocados
- 4 slices of bloomer style bread
- Scrambled Eggs
- 6 eggs
- 50ml single cream
- or whole milk
- 1 tbsp chopped chives, optional
- 10g butter
- 120g smoked salmon,
- roughly chopped
- Salt and black pepper

Directions:

1. Halve the avocado and remove the stone, then use a tablespoon to scoop out the flesh into a mixing bowl. Season with salt and black pepper and smash the flesh with a fork.
2. Set the air fryer temperature to 200°C and place the bread onto the air fryer tray, making sure that the slices are evenly spaced. Toast the bread for 8-10 minutes, depending on how brown you like your toast.
3. Meanwhile, in a jug lightly whisk together the eggs and cream, then stir through the chives and season. Melt the butter in a non-stick frying pan and pour in the eggs. Let the mixture sit for about 30 seconds, then stir with a wooden spoon. Allow to sit again for a few seconds, then stir and fold again, until the eggs are set and scrambled.
4. Stir ¾ of the salmon through the scrambled eggs and season to taste. To assemble, spread the avocado evenly over the toasted bread, top with scrambled eggs and garnish with the remaining salmon.

Nutritional Value (Amount per Serving):

Calories: 661; Fat: 45.21; Carb: 20.42; Protein: 44.15

Sourdough Bruschetta

Prep Time: 5 Mins
Cook Time: 10 Mins   Serves: 4

Ingredients:

- 5 large vine tomatoes
- 1 cloves garlic, crushed
- 1 small bunch basil,
- leaves roughly chopped
- 1 small red onion,
- finely chopped
- 3 tbsps extra virgin olive oil
- 1 tbsp balsamic vinegar
- Sea salt and freshly ground
- black pepper
- 4 slices of sourdough bread
- Salt and black pepper

Directions:

1. Cut the tomatoes in half and, using a teaspoon, remove the seeds and discard. Finely chop the tomatoes and place in a mixing bowl.
2. Add the garlic, ¾ of the basil, red onion, 2 tbsps olive oil and balsamic vinegar. Season with salt and black pepper and mix to combine.
3. Set the air fryer temperature to 200°C and place the bread onto the air fryer tray, making sure that they are evenly spaced. Toast the bread for 8-10 minutes, depending on how brown you like your toast.
4. Drizzle the warm toast with the remaining oil, top with the tomato mixture, then garnish with remaining basil leaves

Nutritional Value (Amount per Serving):

Calories: 563; Fat: 12.86; Carb: 85.25; Protein: 28.07

Air Fryer Chinese Kebabs Rice

Prep Time: 10 Mins
Cook Time: 20 Mins   Serves: 4

Ingredients:

- 100g Egg Fried Rice
- 150g Minced Pork
- ½ Small Onion (peeled and diced)
- 1Tsp Garlic Puree
- 1Tsp Tomato Puree
- 1Tbsp Chinese Five Spice
- 1 Slice Wholemeal Bread (made into breadcrumbs)
- 1Tbsp Soy Sauce
- Salt & Pepper

Directions:

1. Firstly make your egged fried rice. Boil your Chinese rice in a pan and once it is cooked at the same Chinese seasoning as used in the kebab, add a hard boiled egg and mix it well.
2. To make the kebabs place the second half of the seasoning in a mixing bowl. Add the onion and mince and mix well. 3. Add the breadcrumbs and form into sausage shapes.
3. Cook in the Air Fryer for 20 minutes on a 180°C heat.

Nutritional Value (Amount per Serving):

Calories: 175; Fat: 8.89; Carb: 8.92; Protein: 14.15

Two Ingredient Air Fryer Croutons

Prep Time: 3 Mins
Cook Time: 8 Mins   Serves: 9

Ingredients:

- 2 Slices Wholemeal Bread
- 1Tbsp Olive Oil

Directions:

1. Chop your slices of bread into medium chunks and place them in the Air Fryer.
2. Add the olive oil and cook for 8 minutes on a 200°C heat.

3. Serve over your soup or as a snack.

Nutritional Value (Amount per Serving):

Calories: 25; Fat: 1.65; Carb: 2.2; Protein: 0.39

The Ultimate Fried English Breakfast

Prep Time: 2 Mins
Cook Time: 20 Mins   Serves: 4

Ingredients:

- 8 Medium Sausages
- 8 Rashers Unsmoked Back Bacon
- 4 Eggs
- 1 Can Baked Beans
- 8 Slices Toast

Directions:

1. In the Air Fryer place your sausages and bacon in it and cook for 10 minutes on 160°C.
2. In one ramekin place the baked beans and in another your egg (ready for it to be fried).
3. Cook for a further 10 minutes on 200°C until everything is cooked.
4. Dish up and serve.

Nutritional Value (Amount per Serving):

Calories: 409; Fat: 29.51; Carb: 10.44; Protein: 29.11

Traditional Welsh Rarebit Air Fryer Style

Prep Time: 10 Mins
Cook Time: 15 Mins   Serves: 2

Ingredients:

- 3 Slices Bread
- 2 Large Eggs (separated)
- 1Tsp Mustard
- 1Tsp Paprika
- 120g Cheddar

Directions:

1. Very lightly heat up the bread in the Air Fryer so that it is almost like toast. The best way to do this is to give it 5 minutes on 180°C.
2. Whisk the egg whites in a bowl until they form soft peaks.
3. Mix the egg yolks, cheese, paprika and mustard in a bowl.
4. Then fold in the egg whites.
5. Spoon it onto the partly toasted bread and cook in the Air Fryer for 10 minutes on 180°C.
6. Serve!

Nutritional Value (Amount per Serving):

Calories: 383; Fat: 26.03; Carb: 17; Protein: 20.3

Chapter 2: Vegetables

Air Fryer Brussels Sprout Crisps

Prep Time: 5 Mins
Cook Time: 20 Mins   Serves: 2 – 3

Ingredients:

- 225 g brussels sprouts, thinly sliced
- 1 tbsp. extra-virgin olive oil
- 2 tbsp. freshly grated Parmesan, plus more for garnish
- 1 tsp. garlic powder
- Salt
- Freshly ground black pepper
- Caesar dressing, for dipping

Directions:

1. In a large bowl, toss brussels sprouts with oil, Parmesan, and garlic powder and season with salt and pepper. Arrange in an even layer in air fryer.
2. Bake at 180°C for 8 minutes, toss, and bake 8 minutes more, until crisp and golden.
3. Garnish with more Parmesan and serve with caesar dressing for dipping.

Nutritional Value (Amount per Serving):

Calories: 378; Fat: 24.26; Carb: 8.81; Protein: 30.78

Air Fryer Sweet Potato Fries

Prep Time: 15 Mins
Cook Time: 35 Mins   Serves: 2

Ingredients:

- or The Fries
- 2 medium sweet potatoes, peeled and cut into sticks
- 1 tbsp. extra-virgin olive oil
- 1/2 tsp. garlic powder
- 1/2 tsp. chilli powder
- Salt
- Freshly ground black pepper
- or The Dipping Sauce
- 2 tbsp. mayonnaise
- 2 tbsp. barbecue sauce
- 1 tsp. hot sauce

Directions:

1. In a large bowl, toss sweet potatoes with oil and spices. Season with salt and pepper.
2. Working in batches, spread an even layer of sweet potato fries in fryer basket. Cook at 190°C for 8 minutes, flip fries, then cook 8 minutes more.
3. Meanwhile, make dipping sauce: In a medium bowl, whisk to combine mayonnaise, barbecue sauce, and hot sauce.
4. Serve fries with sauce on the side for dipping.

Nutritional Value (Amount per Serving):

Calories: 690; Fat: 40.61; Carb: 35.39; Protein: 43.57

Air Fryer Sliced Potatoes

Prep Time: 10 Mins
Cook Time: 15 Mins   Serves: 4

Ingredients:

- 500 g Potatoes
- 1 teaspoon Paprika
- ½ teaspoon Garlic powder
- ½ teaspoon Onion granules
- ½ teaspoon Parsley
- ½ teaspoon Rosemary or Thyme
- ¼ teaspoon Black pepper or to taste
- Salt to taste
- 1 tablespoon Olive oil

Directions:

1. Peel the potatoes, wash them and pat dry with paper towels. If you prefer not to peel the potatoes, wash the potatoes thoroughly to remove any dirt on the skin then pat dry with kitchen towel.
2. Slice the potatoes into even slices.
3. Transfer the potatoes into a bowl then add in paprika, parsley, rosemary, onion granules, garlic powder, black pepper, salt and olive oil. Mix till all well combined.
4. Pour the potatoes into the air fryer basket and spread them out.
5. Air fry sliced potatoes at a temperature of 180°C for 8 minutes, bring out the basket shake it, and air fry potatoes for another 8 minutes or until the potatoes are tender inside and crispy outside.
6. Bring out the potatoes, and serve.

Nutritional Value (Amount per Serving):

Calories: 131; Fat: 4; Carb: 23; Protein: 3

Air Fryer Vegetables

Prep Time: 10 Mins
Cook Time: 15 Mins   Serves: 4

Ingredients:

- 380 g Broccoli
- 250 g Carrots
- 1 Large Bell pepper
- 1 Large Onion
- ½ teaspoon Black pepper
- 1 tablespoon Olive oil
- 1 teaspoon Seasoning vegetable, chicken, turkey seasoning or any of choice.
- Salt to taste

Directions:

1. Wash and cut the vegetables into bite size.
2. Add them to a bowl and season with salt, black pepper, or any seasoning of choice, and olive oil. Mix so that the veggies are covered in the seasoning.
3. Add the seasoned veggies into the air fryer basket and air fry at a temperature of 175°C for 15 minutes.
4. Toss the veggies in the basket halfway through cooking so that all sides are crisp.
5. When done, take out the basket and serve.

Nutritional Value (Amount per Serving):

Calories: 120; Fat: 4; Carb: 19; Protein: 4

Air Fryer Roasted Garlic

Prep Time: 5 Mins
Cook Time: 30 Mins   Serves: 2

Ingredients:

- 2 garlic bulbs
- 2 Tablespoons Extra virgin olive oil substitute with olive oil, avocado oil, or any other oil of choice
- Salt to taste this is optional

Directions:

1. Preheat your air fryer to 190°C, cut some

aluminum foil sheets that will be enough for the number of garlic heads you will be air frying.
2. Peel the papery outer layer of a garlic head, using a sharp knife cut about ½ inches of the garlic head so that top of all the cloves is exposed. Place each garlic bulb on the prepared foil sheets
3. Drizzle a little bit of olive oil over the garlic, and then sprinkle with salt if using. Wrap the foil around the garlic tightly to form a parcel.
4. Place the wrapped garlic in the air fryer tray, and cook for 20-30 minutes or until the cloves are soft and lightly golden brown.
5. Let the roasted garlic cool slightly before squeezing out the cloves to use in your dishes.

Nutritional Value (Amount per Serving):

Calories: 133; Fat: 13.64; Carb: 2.81; Protein: 0.54

Crispy Roast Potatoes

Prep Time: 5 Mins
Cook Time: 30 Mins   Serves: 4

Ingredients:

- 1kg potatoes, such as Maris
- piper or Desiree, peeled and
- chopped into 4cm chunks
- 1 tbsp plain flour
- 2 tbsp vegetable oil
- Salt and ground
- black pepper

Directions:

1. Bring a large saucepan of water to the boil with a pinch of salt. Add the potatoes to the boiling water and cook for 8-10 minutes until the edges have softened when you poke them with a knife.
2. Drain the potatoes in a colander and return them to the pan, sprinkle on the flour and oil then give the pan a shake to fluff up the potatoes.
3. Carefully transfer the potatoes into the air fryer basket. Set the temperature to 180°C for 20 minutes shaking them halfway through until the potatoes are crisp and golden.

Nutritional Value (Amount per Serving):

Calories: 593; Fat: 24.46; Carb: 46.27; Protein: 45.7

Chapter 3: Poultry

Stuffed Chicken Breast Wrapped In Serrano Ham

Prep Time: 5 Mins
Cook Time: 30 Mins   Serves: 4

Ingredients:

- 4 medium chicken breasts
- 100g soft cheese with
- garlic and herbs
- 4 slices Serrano ham
- Vegetable oil spray
- Salt and black pepper

Directions:

1. Using a sharp knife, cut a pocket in the fattest part of each chicken breast then fill with equal amounts of the cheese. Season the chicken with salt and black pepper.
2. Wrap the chicken breasts with Serrano ham then place on an air flow rack lined with parchment paper and spray lightly with oil.
3. Place the chicken on the air fryer tray and start the chicken program. Check that the chicken breasts are cooked using a meat probe (the temperature should be over 75°C) and extend the cooking time if necessary.
4. Remove the chicken from the air fryer onto a warm plate and cover with foil for 5 minutes to rest before serving with your favourite seasonal vegetables and roast potatoes.

Nutritional Value (Amount per Serving):

Calories: 558; Fat: 29.35; Carb: 3.66; Protein: 66.2

Herby Chicken Thighs

Prep Time: 5 Mins
Cook Time: 30 – 40 Mins   Serves: 2-4

Ingredients:

- 4 chicken thighs, with skin on
- 2 level tsp dried oregano
- 2 level tsp dried thyme
- 2 bay leaves
- black pepper
- 2 tbsp lemon juice
- 5 tbsp olive oil   • A little salt

Directions:

1. Prick the chicken all over with a fork and place in a shallow layer in a dish.
2. Sprinkle on the oregano and thyme, add the bay leaves and a generous grinding of black pepper.
3. Pour on the lemon juice and olive oil and turn the joints to coat them all over.
4. Cover the dish with foil, place in the fridge for at least 4 hours, turning from time to time.
5. Preheat at 180°C for 3 minutes.
6. Discarding the marinade place the chicken into the frying basket.
7. Cook at 180°C for 30 -40 minutes, turning halfway through cooking. Ensure the chicken is fully cooked and that the juices run clear before serving.
8. Season the chicken with a little salt and serve on a bed of watercress with new potatoes or French fries.

Nutritional Value (Amount per Serving):

Calories: 775; Fat: 65.37; Carb: 2.65; Protein: 42.72

Air Fryer Chicken Wrapped In Bacon

Prep Time: 3 Mins
Cook Time: 15 Mins   Serves: 6

Ingredients:

- 6 Rashers Unsmoked Back Bacon
- 1 Small Chicken Breast
- 1Tbsp Garlic Soft Cheese

Directions:

1. Chop up your chicken breast into six bite sized pieces.
2. Lay out your bacon rashers and spread them with a small layer of soft cheese.
3. Place your chicken on top of the cheese and roll them up. Secure them with a cocktail stick.
4. Place them in the Air Fryer for 15 minutes on a 180°C heat.

Nutritional Value (Amount per Serving):

Calories: 99; Fat: 5.98; Carb: 0.32; Protein: 10.64

Air Fryer Prawn Paste Chicken Wings

Prep Time: 10 Mins
Cook Time: 20 Mins   Serves: 3

Ingredients:

- 300g Mid-joint Chicken Wings or Drumlettes
- 2 tablespoon Olive Oil
- 1 tablespoon Prawn/Shrimp Paste
- 3/4 teaspoon Sugar
- 1 teaspoon Sesame Oil
- 1 teaspoon Ginger Juice
- 1/2 teaspoon Chinese Rice Wine / Sherry
- Corn Flour

Directions:

1. In a bowl, combine prawn paste, sugar, sesame oil, ginger juice and rice wine together until a paste is formed. Marinade chicken with the sauce for at least an hour or preferably overnight in the fridge.
2. Coat the marinated chicken with corn flour. Stir to coat evenly, shaking off excess flour on the chicken.
3. Preheat air fryer at 180°C. Meanwhile, lightly brush chicken pieces with olive oil.
4. Place the chickens into the air fryer. Cook for 8 minutes. Pull out the tray, use tongs to turn chicken pieces over, and cook for another 7 minutes. Drain cooked chicken on paper towels before serving.
5. Enjoy.

Nutritional Value (Amount per Serving):

Calories: 323; Fat: 23.38; Carb: 7.68; Protein: 20.14

Air Fryer Grilled Chicken Sticks

Prep Time: 10 Mins
Cook Time: 30 Mins   Serves: 4

Ingredients:

- 8 6" Bamboo Skewer Sticks
- 4 pieces Chicken Thigh Meat
- 1 teaspoon Sugar
- 1 tablespoon Mirin

- 1 teaspoon Garlic Salt
- 60ml Soy Sauce (light)
- 5 Green Onions (spring onions)

Directions:

1. Soak bamboo sticks in water for 15 minutes.
2. Cut chicken into 1" square pieces.
3. Cut green onions into 1" length.
4. Stick chicken & onion in alternate orders into skewers
5. In a mixing bowl, add soy sauce, garlic salt, Mirin & sugar. Mix well.
6. Marinate chicken with sauce for at 2 hours,
7. Preheat air fryer for 5 minutes at 180°C.
8. Place skewers into air fryer and cook for 12 minutes.
9. Enjoy.

Nutritional Value (Amount per Serving):

Calories: 413; Fat: 10.73; Carb: 36.52; Protein: 42.56

Honey Lemon Chicken Stuffed With Zucchini

Prep Time: 10 Mins
Cook Time: 30 Mins   Serves: 4

Ingredients:

- 1 whole chicken
- or The Filling:
- 2 tablespoons olive oil
- 2 red onions
- 1 green zucchini
- 1 yellow zucchini
- 1 sweet apple
- 2 apricots
- Fresh thyme
- or The Marinade:
- 200 g honey
- Juice of 1 large lemon
- Freshly ground pepper
- Salt

Directions:

1. Chop all the ingredients for the filling into small cubes and mix with the oil in a bowl. Season to taste with salt and pepper. Fill the chicken with the mixture.
2. Heat the Air fryer to 200 degrees C. If you have the grill pan accessory you can use this to place the chicken on, so you have more space in your Air fryer. The Viva model fits a chicken of up to 1.2 kg; the Avance model up to

1.6 kg. Place the chicken in the Air fryer and sear the meat for 5 minutes.

3. Meanwhile, melt the honey in a pan with the juice of the lemon and season it to taste with salt and pepper. Take the chicken out of the Air fryer and cover it in some of the marinade. Set the temperature of the Air fryer to 150 degrees and put the chicken back in. Open the Air fryer every 15 minutes to cover the chicken with marinade until it has all gone. After 60 minutes, the chicken will be cooked. There are two ways to check whether the chicken is cooked. Either with a meat thermometer (temperature must be 85 degrees) or by checking the color of the liquid. When cooked, the liquid will run clear and show no pink.

Nutritional Value (Amount per Serving):

Calories: 834; Fat: 22.6; Carb: 59.79; Protein: 99.76

Roasted Chicken Wings

Prep Time: 5 Mins
Cook Time: 10 Mins   Serves: 4

Ingredients:

- 2 cloves garlic
- 1 teaspoon ground cumin
- 500 g chicken wings at room temperature
- 2 teaspoons ginger powder
- Freshly ground black pepper
- 100 ml sweet chili sauce

Directions:

1. Preheat the Air Fryer to 180°C.
2. Mix the garlic with the ginger powder, cumin, plenty of freshly ground black pepper and some salt. Rub the chicken wings with the herbs.
3. Put the chicken wings in the basket and slide it into the Air Fryer. Set the timer to 10 minutes and roast the chicken wings until they are crispy brown.
4. Serve the chicken wings with the chili sauce as a main course or a snack.

Nutritional Value (Amount per Serving):

Calories: 527; Fat: 32.3; Carb: 10.03; Protein: 45.52

Spicy Drumsticks With Barbecue Marinade

Prep Time: 25 Mins
Cook Time: 20 Mins   Serves: 4

Ingredients:

- 1 clove garlic, crushed
- ½ tablespoon mustard
- 2 teaspoons brown sugar
- 1 teaspoon chili powder
- Freshly ground black pepper
- 1 tablespoon olive oil   • 4 drumsticks

Directions:

1. Preheat the Air Fryer to 200°C.
2. Mix the garlic with the mustard, brown sugar, chili powder, a pinch of salt and freshly ground pepper to taste. Mix with the oil.
3. Rub the drumsticks completely with the marinade and leave to marinate for 20 minutes.
4. Put the drumsticks in the basket and slide the basket into the Air Fryer. Set the timer to 10 minutes. Roast the drumsticks until brown.
5. Then lower the temperature to 150°C and roast the drumsticks for another 10 minutes until done.
6. Serve the drumsticks with corn salad and French bread.

Nutritional Value (Amount per Serving):

Calories: 275; Fat: 19.81; Carb: 2.88; Protein: 20.54

Air Fryer Chicken Fried Rice

Prep Time: 5 Mins
Cook Time: 20 Mins   Serves: 6

Ingredients:

- 325g rice cold
- 130g chicken leftover and cubed
- 5 tbsp tamari soy sauce or regular if not gluten free
- 200g frozen veggies (I used sweet corn and peas)
- 2 green onions (spring onions), sliced
- 1 tsp sesame oil

- 1 tsp vegetable oil
- 1 tbsp chili sauce optional
- salt to taste

Directions:

1. Preheat the air fryer to 180°C.
2. Mix all the ingredients together in a large bowl.
3. Then transfer to a non-stick pan that fits inside the air fryer basket.
4. Cook for 20 minutes, stirring the rice mixture a couple of times during cooking.

Nutritional Value (Amount per Serving):

Calories: 104; Fat: 3.41; Carb: 15.69; Protein: 2.97

Crispy Air Fryer Chicken Breast (Healthier And Juicy)

Prep Time: 5 Mins
Cook Time: 10 Mins   Serves: 4

Ingredients:

- 450g skinless boneless chicken breasts halved crossways
- 50g gluten-free breadcrumbs or regular
- 4 tbsp grated parmesan cheese
- 1 tsp paprika
- 1 tsp Italian seasoning
- salt optional
- ½ tsp ground coriander
- cooking spray

Directions:

1. Preheat the air fryer to 180°C.
2. Mix together breadcrumbs, parmesan cheese, paprika, Italian Seasoning, ground coriander and salt in a bowl.
3. Lightly spray both sides of the halved chicken breast with a calorie-controlled cooking spray.
4. Cover both sides of the chicken breasts with the coating mix and place chicken breast in the air fryer basket. Make sure the chicken breasts are not touching.
5. Cook between 4-5 minutes then flip over and cook for 4-5 minutes on the next side. " Cooking times depending on the thickness of the breast so maybe a little more or a little less. Chicken is done when it reaches an internal temperature of 75°C.
6. Air Fryers vary in their temperatures which is why I have added a cooking time range. When cooking this for the first time start with the lowest cooking times and adjust accordingly.

Nutritional Value (Amount per Serving):

Calories: 208; Fat: 4.71; Carb: 11.99; Protein: 27.87

Chapter 4: Meats

Air Fryer Party Meatballs

Prep Time: 20 Mins
Cook Time: 15 Mins   Serves: 24

Ingredients:

- 500g Mince Beef
- 50g Tomato Ketchup
- 1Tbsp Tabasco
- 21/2 Tbsp Worcester Sauce
- 60g Vinegar
- 1Tbsp Lemon Juice
- 50g Brown Sugar
- ½ Tsp Dry Mustard
- 3 Gingersnaps (crushed)

Directions:

1. In a large mixing bowl place on your seasonings and mix well so that everything is evenly coated.
2. Add the mince to the bowl and mix well.
3. Form into medium sized meatballs and place them into your Air Fryer.
4. Cook them for 15 minutes on a 190°C heat or until nice and crispy and cooked in the middle.
5. Place them on sticks before serving.

Nutritional Value (Amount per Serving):

Calories: 56; Fat: 1.61; Carb: 5.79; Protein: 4.66

Air Fryer Scallops With Cheese

Prep Time: 15 Mins
Cook Time: 10 Mins   Serves: 2

Ingredients:

- 5 Half-shelled Scallops
- 30g Butter (cubed, unsalted)
- 2 tablespoon Mayonnaise
- Salt
- Black Pepper
- 60g Shredded Mozzarella Cheese

Directions:

1. Preheat air fryer at 200°C.

2. Remove scallop meat from the shell, rinse the meat thoroughly and remove any dirty bits. Scald the scallop shells in hot water for a few minutes to disinfect, discard hot water and rinse the shells. Return scallop meat to the shell.
3. Place cubed butter in a small bowl and microwave for 40 seconds. Use a spoon to stir the butter vigorously to form a smooth paste. Add mayonnaise, salt and pepper; stir to combine well.
4. Place scallops on foil and place them into the air fryer. Cook for 5 minutes.
5. Using kitchen tongs, carefully drain the scallop broth collected in the shells in a small bowl.
6. Divide and spoon the mayonnaise mixture evenly among the scallops. Top with shredded cheese.
7. Return scallops to the air fryer and cook for another 8 minutes, or until the cheese is melted and slightly browned at the edges.

Nutritional Value (Amount per Serving):

Calories: 188; Fat: 13.54; Carb: 4.8; Protein: 11.85

Air Fryer Roast Pork

Prep Time: 10 Mins
Cook Time: 50 Mins   Serves: 3

Ingredients:

- 600g Pork Belly
- 1/3 tablespoon Shaoxing Wine (or Dry Sherry)
- 2 teaspoon Salt
- 1 1/2 teaspoon Sugar
- 1/2 teaspoon Five-spice Powder

Directions:

1. Use a knife to scrape away any impurities and hair from the pork belly. Rinse thoroughly.
2. Prepare the seasonings by combining salt with sugar and five-spice powder well.
3. Blanch pork belly in boiling water for about 12 minutes, or until 60% done, and the skin is softened.
4. Drain well and wipe dry.
5. Cut a few slits on the meat to help absorb seasonings better.
6. Rub wine and seasoning evenly on pork. Make sure there's no seasonings on the rind, otherwise the five-spice powder will darken it.
7. Turn over, and wipe dry the rind. Use a fork to poke the rind as many holes

as possible.
8. Wrap the pork meat with foil and leave the rind unwrapped. Place in fridge, let air dry overnight in fridge.
9. Remove pork from fridge and let it rest in room temperature.
10. Poke the rind with fork evenly once again. Wipe dry.
11. Preheat the air fryer for 5 minutes at 160°C.
12. Place the pork belly skin facing up into the air-fryer. Cook for 160°C for 15 minutes.
13. Take out and wipe dry the rind again. Continue at 180°C for 30 minutes.
14. Chopped into small bite-sized pieces.

Nutritional Value (Amount per Serving):

Calories: 1046; Fat: 106.02; Carb: 2.59; Protein: 18.73

Spicy Country Fries

Prep Time: 10 Mins
Cook Time: 20 Mins   Serves: 4

Ingredients:

- 800 g waxy potatoes
- 2 small, dried chilies or 1 heaped teaspoon freshly ground, dried chili flakes
- ½ tablespoon freshly ground black pepper
- 1 tablespoon olive oil

Directions:

1. Preheat the Air Fryer to 180°C.
2. Scrub the potatoes clean under running water. Cut them lengthwise into 1½ cm strips.
3. Soak the fries in water for at least 30 minutes. Drain them thoroughly and then pat them dry with kitchen paper.
4. Crush the chilies very finely (in a mortar) and mix them in a bowl with the olive oil, pepper and curry powder. Coat the fries with this mixture.
5. Transfer the fries to the fryer basket and slide the basket into the Air Fryer. Set the timer to 20 minutes and fry the fries until they are golden brown and done. Turn them every now and again.
6. Serve the fries in a platter and sprinkle with salt. Delicious with steak.

Nutritional Value (Amount per Serving):

Calories: 765; Fat: 44.19; Carb: 34.94; Protein: 54.3

Frozen Bacon In Air Fryer

Prep Time: 5 Mins
Cook Time: 20 Mins   Serves: 4

Ingredients:

- 620 g Frozen Back Bacon

Directions:

1. Remove frozen bacon from the packaging and load into the air fryer basket.
2. Air fry for 8 minutes at 100°C. Turn every 2 minutes and strip the top and bottom slice and move each separated slice to a plate. Until you have all bacon rashers separated. As you do this you will be able to lose any bits of packaging that have also stuck to the bacon.
3. Load the defrosted bacon back into the air fryer basket and spread it out. Air fry for 6 minutes at 200°C turn with tongs and then air fry for the same time and temp on the other side.
4. Air fry for a little longer at 200°C if it is not crispy enough as it will vary depending on the thickness of your bacon and how much you are air frying. Air fry for a little longer at 200°C if it is not crispy enough as it will vary depending on the thickness of your bacon and how much you are air frying.

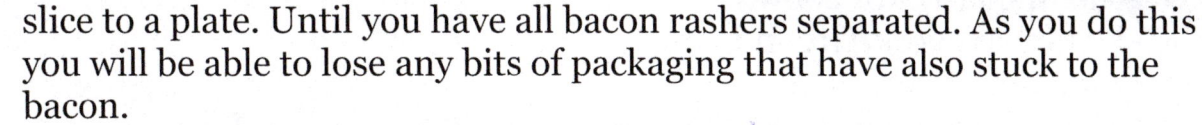

Nutritional Value (Amount per Serving):

Calories: 481; Fat: 45.76; Carb: 9.8; Protein: 16.55

Air Fryer Ground Beef

Prep Time: 2 Mins
Cook Time: 9 Mins   Serves: 2

Ingredients:

- 500 g Ground Beef/Minced Beef
- 1 Tsp Frozen Chopped Garlic
- 1 Tsp Parsley
- Salt & Pepper

Directions:

1. Load into the air fryer basket your block of ground beef.
2. Sprinkle on the top the chopped garlic, salt, pepper, and parsley.

3. Air fry for 9 minutes at 180°C. Though on the 3rd and the 6th minute break up the ground beef so that it has an even cook as it is air frying.
4. When the air fryer beeps drain the liquid from the bottom, and you now have perfectly cooked ground beef ready for adding to meals.

Nutritional Value (Amount per Serving):

Calories: 547; Fat: 27.84; Carb: 2.73; Protein: 66.99

Air Fryer Thai Meatballs

Prep Time: 5 Mins
Cook Time: 10 Mins   Serves: 2

Ingredients:

- Soup Maker Lentil Soup
- 1 kg Minced Pork/Ground Pork
- ½ Medium Red Onion
- 1 Tbsp Philadelphia Light Herbs
- 2 Tsp Garlic Puree
- 1 Tbsp Thai 7 Spice Seasoning
- ½ Tsp Ground Ginger
- 5 Kaffir Lime Leaves
- Salt & Pepper

Directions:

1. Peel and thinly dice your red onion. Thinly slice your Thai leaves.
2. Load into a bowl all your meatball ingredients and mix with your hands for a well coating of the seasoning and the onion.
3. Make into Thai balls using the measuring scales to get equal sized meatballs. We did our meatballs to 47g each.
4. Do all meatballs and then cook them in batches to what will fit in your air fryer.
5. Load the Thai meatballs into the air fryer basket and air fry for 10 minutes at 180°C.
6. When the air fryer beeps serve your Thai meatballs over your lentil soup before serving.

Nutritional Value (Amount per Serving):

Calories: 1016; Fat: 68.58; Carb: 34.12; Protein: 67.87

Air Fryer Pigs in Blanket

Prep Time: 1 Min
Cook Time: 8 Mins   Serves: 4

Ingredients:

- 4 rasher Streaky bacon
- 8 Chipolatas

Directions:

1. Slice the bacon in half.
2. Place the sausages at one end of each of the bacon rashers.
3. Roll the bacon around the sausages.
4. Spray the air fryer basket with some oil and place the pigs in blankets into it. Cook at 180°C for 8 minutes.

Nutritional Value (Amount per Serving):

Calories: 233; Fat: 2.36; Carb: 51.09; Protein: 2.17

Air Fryer Roast Beef

Prep Time: 5 Mins
Cook Time: 45 Mins   Serves: 4

Ingredients:

- easoning
- 2 tsp coarse salt
- 1 tsp freshly ground black pepper
- ½ tsp dried thyme
- ½ tsp garlic granules
- ½ tsp dried rosemary
- ½ tsp mustard powder or brown sugar
- or The Roast Beef
- 1.2 kg roasting beef joint check it fits into your Air fryer
- 3 tbsp olive oil

Directions:

1. Take your beef joint out of the fridge and pat dry. Leave it to come to room temperature for 30 minutes. Make sure to check whether your joint fits into the air fryer. You can always slice a larger joint in half.
2. Meanwhile, preheat the air fryer 200°C for 10 minutes. Mix all the seasoning ingredients together and brush the beef all over with olive oil.

Press the seasoning mix all over the beef.
3. Use a liner in the air fryer basket (optional) and position the beef on top. Roast for 10-15 minutes. Cooking the beef at a high temperature will create a lovely crust on the exterior, sealing all the lovely juices within in the same way that searing the beef in a skillet before roasting in the oven.
4. Remove the air fryer basket and turn the beef over. Reduce the temperature to 180°C and cook for a further 30 minutes.
5. Start checking the internal temperature of the beef with an instant read thermometer inserting the probe in the middle thickest part. Use the table in the recipe notes as a guide to cook it to your liking, adding five minutes of cooking time until your preferred temperature is reached. Remember that the temperature of the joint will continue to rise slightly as it rests so factor that in. I usually aim for medium rare (55-57°C).
6. Once the beef is cooked to your liking place it on a warm platter and cover loosely with foil. Leave it to rest for 20-30 minutes before slicing against the grain and serving with your favorite side dishes.

Nutritional Value (Amount per Serving):

Calories: 679; Fat: 37.6; Carb: 3.49; Protein: 76.75

Frozen Meatballs In Air Fryer

Prep Time: 1 Min
Cook Time: 15 Mins   Serves: 4

Ingredients:

- 1 package frozen meatballs any type
- cooking oil or oil spray

Directions:

1. Remove your frozen meatballs from their outer packaging.
2. Place the frozen meatballs in the air fryer basket in an even layer. Spray the meatballs with cooking oil.
3. Air Fry at 180°C for 12-15 minutes, until the meatballs are heated through.
4. Serve immediately.

Nutritional Value (Amount per Serving):

Calories: 207; Fat: 1.73; Carb: 48.08; Protein: 12.11

Chapter 5: Casseroles, Frittatas, and Quiches

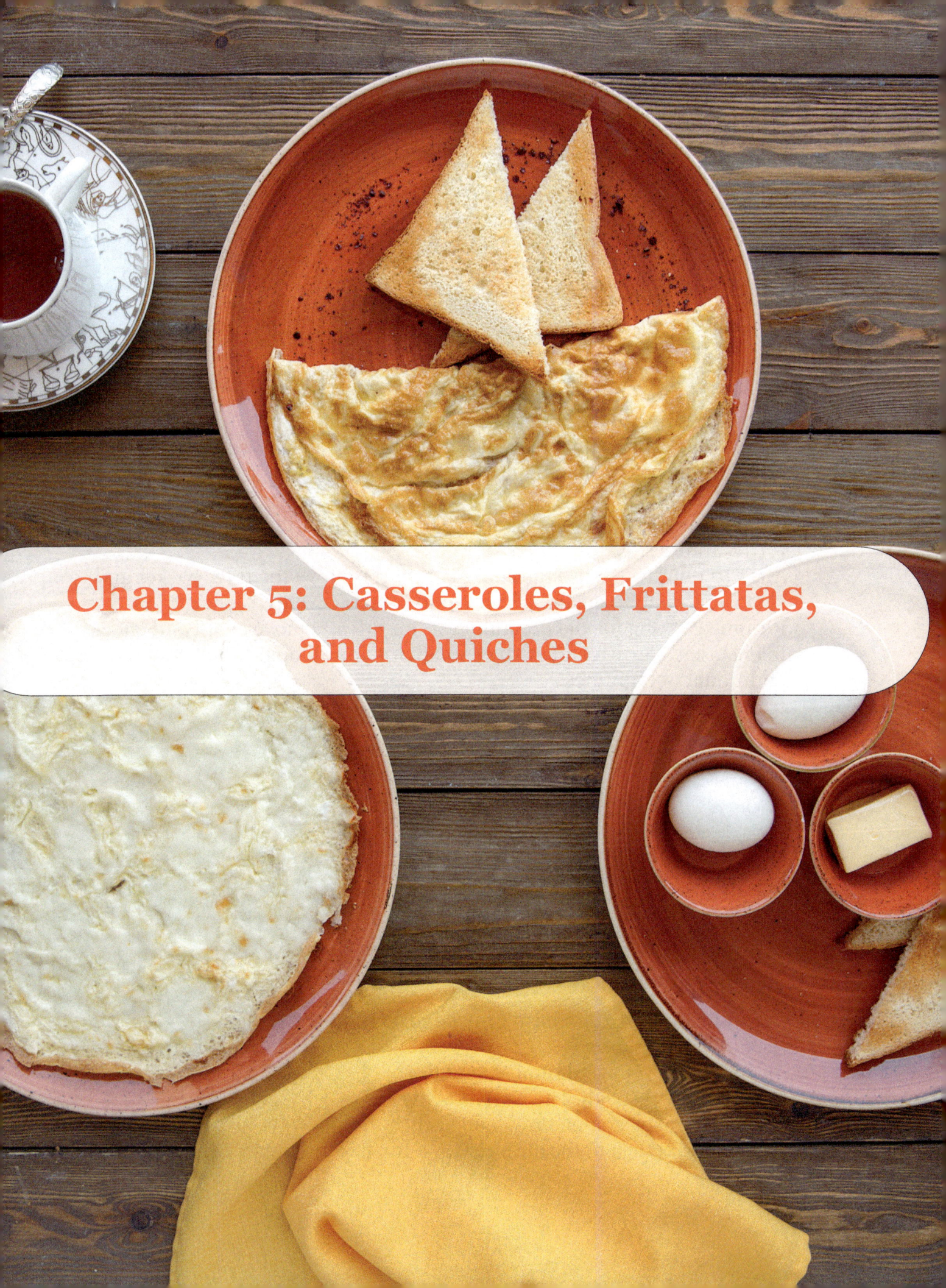

Air Fryer Frozen Samosa

Prep Time: 5 Mins
Cook Time: 20 Mins   Serves: 2

Ingredients:

- Air fryer
- 4 frozen samosas
- Olive oil spray

Directions:

1. Spray both sides of the samosas with olive oil and place them in the air fryer. Do not stack them, if you have a lot of samosas to cook, do them in batches instead of stacking.
2. Set the timer to 20 minutes and the temperature to 190°C and let it cook for 10 minutes.
3. After 10 minutes, pause the cooking timer, remove the fryer basket and shake it around to ensure all the samosas cook evenly.
4. Resume cooking for the remaining 10 minutes, remove again and check to ensure it's brown and crispy enough for your liking. If not, cook for an additional 2-3 minutes.

Nutritional Value (Amount per Serving):

Calories: 198; Fat: 16.24; Carb: 12.25; Protein: 1.7

Air Fryer Frozen Hash Browns

Prep Time: 1 Min
Cook Time: 15 Mins   Serves: 8

Ingredients:

- 8 frozen hash browns

Directions:

1. Add individually frozen hash browns to the air fryer basket.
2. Air fry at 180°C for 15 minutes, and flip over halfway through. The hash browns should be crispy golden brown on each side. If not, return to the air fryer for a further minute or two.

Nutritional Value (Amount per Serving):

Calories: 62; Fat: 3.29; Carb: 8.08; Protein: 0.75

Air Fryer Rhubarb Crumble

Prep Time: 5 Mins
Cook Time: 15 Mins   Serves: 4

Ingredients:

- For the filling:
- 150 g white sugar
- 20 g all purpose plain flour
- 1/2 teaspoon of vanilla extract
- 500 g of rhubarb
- Spray oil or butter to grease ramekins
- For the topping:
- 120 g all purpose plain flour
- 80 g cold butter cut into cubes
- 1/8 teaspoon of salt
- 60 g of light brown sugar

Directions:

1. Pre-heat your air fryer, if required, to 190°C.
2. Get yourself a large mixing bowl.
3. Combine together the white sugar, plain flour and vanilla extract.
4. Wash the rhubarb and remove the ends. Cut into 1/2 inch thick pieces.
5. Add the rhubarb to your filling mixture.
6. Stir well.
7. Place into the lightly greased ramekins.
8. Combine together the flour and butter, til you have a crumble consistency.
9. Add the salt and brown sugar and mix well.
10. Place this over the top of your filling.
11. Bake at 190°C for 15 minutes.
12. Serve with lashings of custard and enjoy!

Nutritional Value (Amount per Serving):

Calories: 775; Fat: 22.74; Carb: 118.16; Protein: 29.14

Air Fryer Tortilla Pizza

Prep Time: 1 Min
Cook Time: 5 Mins   Serves: 1

Ingredients:

- 1 to rtilla
- 30 ml Pizza sauce
- Pepperoni or other toppings
- 30 g grated mozzarella cheese
- Herbs

Directions:

1. Place your tortilla on a chopping board.
2. Spread pizza sauce over the tortilla. If you don't have this in you can use a little passata and tomato puree mixed together OR even just use tomato puree and jazz it up with a little garlic powder, basil and oregano.
3. Add the meat or other pizza toppings.
4. Add the cheese last.
5. Either line the air fryer with baking paper, to prevent sticking, or use a spray oil to spray the entire air fryer basket. I prefer to use baking paper, as it catches the mess and is very simple to remove from the basket with a spatula. I also use spray olive oil, though you're technically not meant to use this in the air fryer!
6. There is no need to pre-heat the air fryer for this recipe.
7. Cook at 200°C for 5 minutes.
8. Top with a sprinkling of fresh herbs (or dried work well too).
9. Slice, serve and enjoy! It goes GREAT with air fryer garlic bread too. Alternatively see below for some other great serving suggestions.

Nutritional Value (Amount per Serving):

Calories: 956; Fat: 32.49; Carb: 119.76; Protein: 45.28

Air Fryer Grilled Ham And Cheese

Prep Time: 2 Mins
Cook Time: 10 Mins   Serves: 1

Ingredients:

- 2 slices of crusty bread
- 40 g sliced or grated cheddar cheese
- 2 slices of cooked ham of choice
- 10 g margarine or mayonnaise your choice

Directions:

1. Pre-heat the air fryer basket to 180°C for 1-2 minutes.
2. Take your bread, layer up the cheese and ham. I like to use sliced ham and sliced cheese for convenience, but you can see below for some other tasty suggestions.
3. Make a sandwich up.
4. Spread the outside of the bread with the butter or mayonnaise.
5. Cook for 10 minutes at 180°C and turn 5 minutes in. You CAN skip the flipping if you're short on time or effort as this only makes a very marginal difference to the cooking and browning of this sandwich.
6. Serve the grilled ham and cheese with your choice of crisps or even a nice side salad to make it a little more balanced.

Nutritional Value (Amount per Serving):

Calories: 295; Fat: 14.47; Carb: 24.57; Protein: 16.7

Air Fryer Chimichanga

Prep Time: 15 Mins
Cook Time: 35 Mins   Serves: 8

Ingredients:

- 1 tbsp. extra-virgin olive oil
- 1 small yellow onion, chopped
- 2 cloves garlic, crushed
- 1 tsp. chilli powder
- 1 tsp. ground cumin
- 1/2 tsp. garlic powder
- 195 g salsa
- 560 g shredded cooked chicken

- Salt
- Freshly ground black pepper
- 1 x 400g can refried beans
- 120 g sour cream, plus more for serving
- Cooking spray
- 8 large flour tortillas
- 100 g grated cheddar
- 100 g grated pepper jack cheese
- Guacamole, for serving

Directions:

1. In a medium pan over medium heat, heat oil. Add onions and cook until soft, 5 minutes. Add garlic, chilli powder, cumin, and garlic powder. Cook until fragrant, 1 minute. Add salsa and bring to a simmer, then add shredded chicken and toss to coat. Season with salt and pepper. Remove from heat.
2. Spread about 65g of refried beans in centre of tortilla, then sprinkle with both cheeses. Top with about 70g of chicken mixture and some sour cream. Roll into a burrito by folding the top and bottom of tortilla into the centre, then fold the right side all the way over the filling, tucking and rolling tightly. Set aside on a plate, seam side down, and repeat with remaining tortillas and filling.
3. Working in batches as necessary, place burritos into basket of air fryer, seam side down, and spray with a little cooking spray. Cook at 200°C for 5 minutes, then flip, spray with more cooking spray, and cook another 5 minutes.
4. Drizzle with more sour cream and serve with guacamole.

Nutritional Value (Amount per Serving):

Calories: 783; Fat: 52.21; Carb: 28.95; Protein: 47.66

Air Fryer Omelette

Prep Time: 5 Mins
Cook Time: 15 Mins   Serves: 2

Ingredients:

- 4 Eggs
- 2 tablespoons Whole Milk
- 1 Tomato chopped
- 2 sprig Spring onions chopped
- ½ teaspoon Seasoning
- ¼ teaspoon Black pepper
- Salt to taste
- ¼ cup Chopped Cooked Meat- chicken, beef, sausage Optional
- Cheese Optional

Directions:

1. In a bowl, break the eggs then add milk. Whisk till well mixed.
2. Add in salt, black pepper, chopped spring onions, tomatoes, and seasoning, Mix together.
3. Grease or spray the pan with cooking oil or butter. This is so the Omelette comes out clean from the pan.
4. Now, pour the egg mixture into the baking pan.
5. Place the pan in the air fryer basket and air fry at a temperature of 140°C for 10 minutes or till cooked through and a toothpick inserted comes out clean.
6. Take the pan out, turn onto a plate.
7. cut up, serve and enjoy your Omelette frittata.

Nutritional Value (Amount per Serving):

Calories: 154; Fat: 9; Carb: 6; Protein: 12

Cheese And Spring Onion Quesadilla

Prep Time: 5 Mins
Cook Time: 12 Mins   Serves: 4

Ingredients:

- 200g cheddar cheese, grated
- 3 tbsps mayonnaise
- 4 spring onions, finely chopped
- 4 x 20cm soft tortilla wraps
- 1 egg, beaten
- 1 tbsp olive oil
- Salt and black pepper
- 4 portions mixed salad

Directions:

1. Place the grated cheese, mayonnaise and spring onions in a bowl, season with salt and black pepper and mix well to combine.
2. Lay the wraps on a flat surface, brush the edges with egg, then divide the cheese mixture evenly between the wraps. Fold the wraps over like a pasty and press the edges down firmly to seal.
3. Brush the wraps lightly with oil. Set the air fryer temperature to 200°C and place the quesadilla onto the basket, making sure that they are evenly spaced. Toast for 10-12 minutes, until the quesadillas are crisp and golden.
4. Cut each quesadilla in half and serve warm with a portion of salad.

Nutritional Value (Amount per Serving):

Calories: 425; Fat: 21.86; Carb: 32.3; Protein: 24

Easy Sage Onion Stuffing Balls

Prep Time: 3 Mins
Cook Time: 15 Mins   Serves: 9

Ingredients:

- 100g Sausage Meat
- ½ Small Onion (peeled and diced)
- ½ Tsp Garlic Puree
- 1Tsp Sage
- 3Tbsp Breadcrumbs
- Salt & Pepper

Directions:

1. Place your ingredients into a mixing bowl and mix well.
2. Form into medium sized balls and place them in the Air Fryer
3. Cook at 180°C for 15 minutes and then serve.

Nutritional Value (Amount per Serving):

Calories: 73; Fat: 2.55; Carb: 9.46; Protein: 3.52

Courgette Fritters

Prep Time: 10 Mins
Cook Time: 15 Mins   Serves: 9

Ingredients:

- 100g Plain Flour
- 1 Medium Egg (beaten)
- 5Tbsp Milk
- 150g Grated Courgette
- 75g Onion (peeled and diced)
- 25g Cheddar Cheese (grated)
- 1Tbsp Mixed Herbs
- Salt & Pepper

Directions:

1. Put the plain flour into a bowl and add the seasoning.
2. Whisk the egg and milk and then add to the flour to make a smooth creamy batter.
3. Grate the courgette making sure to remove any excess moisture. Then add the onion.

4. Stir in the cheese.
5. If the batter isn't very thick then add more flour and cheese to it until it is of a reasonable thick mixture.
6. Make them into small burger shapes and place in the Air Fryer.
7. Cook on a 200°C heat for 20 minutes or until fully cooked.
8. Serve them with a good dollop of sour cream or mayonnaise.

Nutritional Value (Amount per Serving):

Calories: 131; Fat: 5.65; Carb: 12.66; Protein: 7.29

Air Fryer Egg And Bacon Pie

Prep Time: 10 Mins
Cook Time: 20 Mins   Serves: 8

Ingredients:

- Air Fryer Pie Crust
- Air Fryer Frozen Bacon
- 9 Large Eggs
- 4 Tbsp Skimmed Milk
- 2 Tsp Parsley
- Salt & Pepper
- Flour for dusting
- 1 Small Egg beaten

Directions:

1. Place your just cooked bacon on kitchen towels and allow the extra fat to soak into the towels. After 20 minutes remove the bacon and slice into chunks.
2. Flour a clean worktop and a rolling pin and then roll out your shortcrust pastry. Line a quiche dish with shortcrust pastry and then add your bacon bits, spreading them out so that you will get an equal bacon spread.
3. In a jug add the eggs and seasonings and then beat and then add in the milk and carry on stirring.
4. Pour the egg and milk mixture over the bacon until you have an almost full quiche dish.
5. Then roll out the rest of the pastry and line the top of your egg and bacon pie. Then brush on some egg wash and cut a few holes in the centre to allow the pie to breathe as it cooks. Load into the air fryer.
6. Air fry your egg and bacon pie for 20 minutes at 170°C and then keep it in the air fryer to set for a further 20 minutes. Then you can remove the pie from the air fryer, slice and serve.

Nutritional Value (Amount per Serving):

Calories: 180; Fat: 11.97; Carb: 12.53; Protein: 5.48

Chapter 6: Appetizers and Snacks

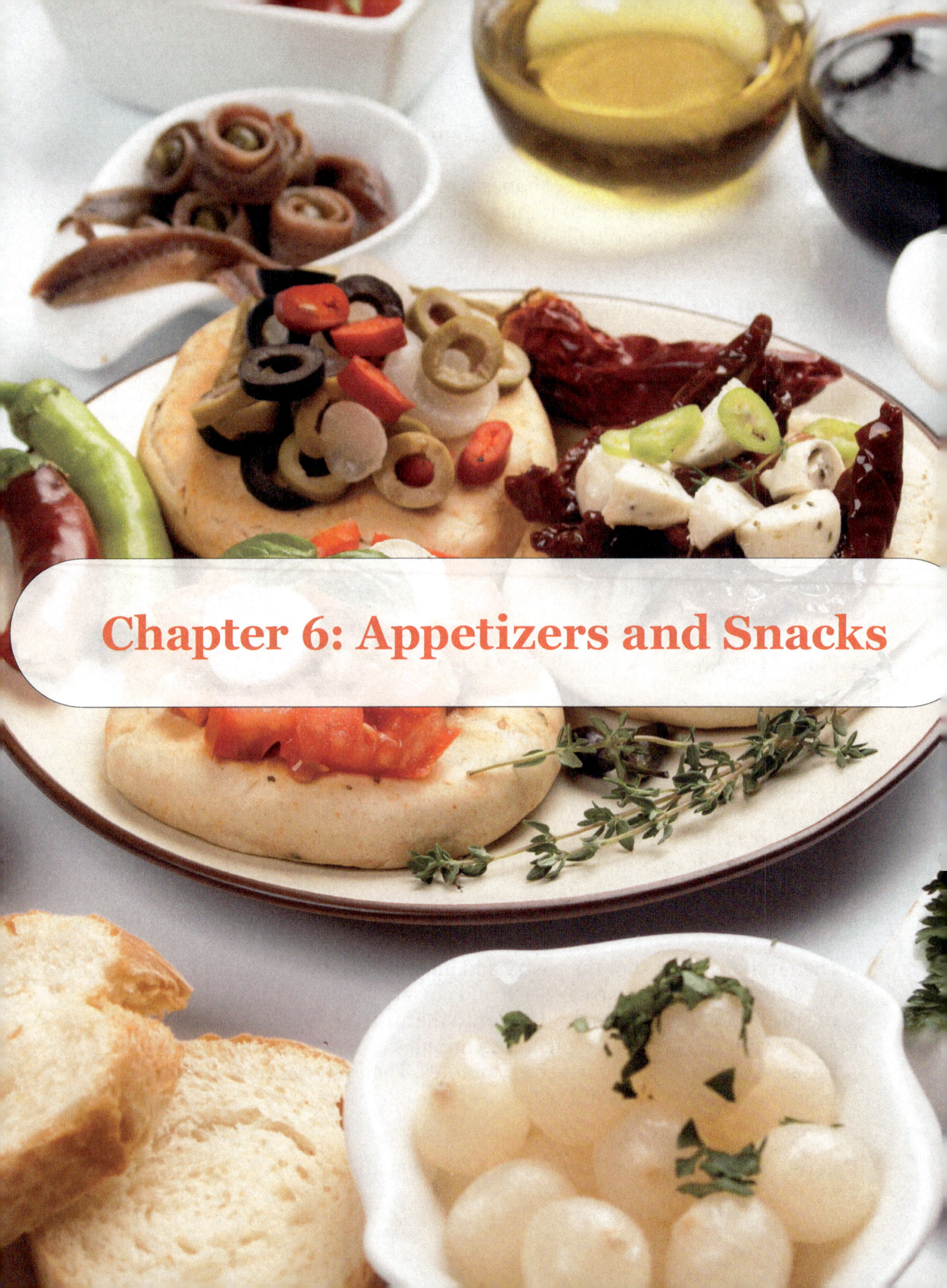

Air Fryer Chicken Kebabs

Prep Time: 10 Minutes
Cook Time: 20 Minutes   Serves: 8

Ingredients:

- 400 g chicken breast or thigh
- 2 white or red onion your choice
- 3 peppers bell peppers
- 150 ml bbq sauce or other sauce of choice
- Salt and pepper

Directions:

1. Cut the chicken breast lengthways into 1 inch thick strips.
2. Cut the onion into quarters. Remove the smallest centre pieces.
3. De-seed the peppers and cut into large chunks, around 1 inch.
4. Place the chicken into a bowl, add the BBQ sauce (or other sauce) and then place into the fridge for a minimum of 1 hour.
5. Layer up your skewers. I like to do pepper, chicken breast, onion, pepper, chicken breast, onion and repeat.
6. I place the chicken on to the skewer in an "S" formation, which I achieve by skewering the bottom of the chicken strip, then the middle folded over, then I fold again and skewer the top of the chicken breast.
7. I place the skewers into the air fryer basket and then cook at 200°C for 20 minutes. At the 10 minute mark I spray lightly with spray oil to keep them from becoming dry.
8. You can use wooden skewers if you don't have a kebab rack, or don't want to buy one, but soak them first to avoid them burning in air fryer.

Nutritional Value (Amount per Serving):

Calories: 439; Fat: 15.79; Carb: 63.36; Protein: 19.14

Air Fryer Frozen Chicken Nuggets

Prep Time: 3 Mins
Cook Time: 10 Mins   Serves: 5

Ingredients:

- 30 frozen chicken nuggets

Directions:

1. Preheat the air fryer to 200°C for 3-5 minutes.
2. Place frozen chicken nuggets in the air fryer basket, spreading them out in a single layer. No need to spray with oil.
3. Air fry the frozen chicken nuggets for 8-10 minutes at 200°C shaking the basket or flipping the nuggets halfway through (optional) until golden brown and cooked through.
4. Remove from the air fryer and serve with your favorite dipping sauce.

Nutritional Value (Amount per Serving):

Calories: 1051; Fat: 72.14; Carb: 49; Protein: 51.59

Reheat French Fries In Fryer

Prep Time: 0 Min
Cook Time: 5 Mins   Serves: 1

Ingredients:

- Leftover french fries
- Dipping sauce of choice to serve

Directions:

1. Preheat the air fryer at 180°C for 3 minutes.
2. Add the leftover to the air fryer basket in a single layer (avoid overcrowding the air fryer for a great result).
3. Reheat the fries at 180°C for 3-5 minutes shaking the air fryer basket halfway through the cooking for even cooking.
4. Serve your reheated fries with any dipping sauce of choice and enjoy.

Nutritional Value (Amount per Serving):

Calories: 14; Fat: 0.43; Carb: 2.3; Protein: 0.29

Dino Nuggets In Air Fryer

Prep Time: 0 Min
Cook Time: 15 Mins   Serves: 4

Ingredients:

- 500g frozen dino nuggets
- dipping sauce of choice

Directions:

1. Remove the frozen dinosaur nuggets from the packaging and arrange them in the air fryer basket, making sure you are not stacking them.
2. Cook the nuggets for 8-10 minutes until crispy and golden on the outside, flipping the basket or flipping the nuggets halfway through
3. Serve immediately with a side of fries, mashed potatoes, veggies and dipping sauce of choice

Nutritional Value (Amount per Serving):

Calories: 159; Fat: 4.5; Carb: 27; Protein: 3.75

Air Fryer Prawns

Prep Time: 5 Mins
Cook Time: 5 Mins   Serves: 4

Ingredients:

- 35g Plain Flour
- 3/4 tsp Garlic Granules
- 1/2 tsp Smoked Paprika
- 1/2 tsp Cayenne
- 1/2 tsp Salt
- 35g Breadcrumbs
- 30g Panko Breadcrumbs
- 2 Eggs, beaten
- 300g Prawns, shelled
- Cooking spray

Directions:

1. Combine flour with 1/2 tsp Garlic, 1/4 tsp Smoked Paprika, 1/4 tsp Cayenne and 1/4 tsp Salt in a bowl.
2. Combine both breadcrumbs with 1/4 tsp Garlic, 1/4 tsp Smoked Paprika, 1/4 tsp Cayenne and 1/4 tsp Salt in another bowl.

3. Preheat air fryer to 200°C.
4. Toss Prawns in the flour mixture.
5. Then dip individually in egg and then breadcrumbs.
6. Repeat with remaining Prawns.
7. Lightly spray with cooking spray.
8. Add a single layer of Prawns to the air fryer basket.
9. Cook for 3 minutes.
10. Flip the Prawns and spray with more oil.
11. Cook for a further 2 – 3 minutes or until just cooked.
12. Repeat with remaining Prawns.

Nutritional Value (Amount per Serving):

Calories: 499; Fat: 21.87; Carb: 63.35; Protein: 11.75

Air Fryer Potatoes

Prep Time: 5 Mins
Cook Time: 22 Mins   Serves: 4

Ingredients:

- 5 Large Potatoes, peeled and cut into 3cm cubes
- Salt
- 2-3 tbsp Oil

Directions:

1. Bring a pot of water to a boil and carefully add Potatoes and a good pinch of Salt.
2. Boil for 12 minutes.
3. Preheat unit and select Air Fryer mode. Set the temperature to 200°C and the timer to 10 minutes.
4. Then drain in a colander. Shake and then add to the unit once ready. Drizzle over the oil. Air fry 10 – 15 minutes. Check if they are cooked through before serving. Season with more salt if needed.

Nutritional Value (Amount per Serving):

Calories: 430; Fat: 8.92; Carb: 80.58; Protein: 9.32

Air Fryer Pitta Pizza

Prep Time: 5 Mins
Cook Time: 8 Mins   Serves: 4

Ingredients:

- 4 gluten free pitta breads
- 4 tbsp (60ml) gluten free bbq sauce
- 80g grated cheddar cheese
- 80g diced mozzarella
- 60g diced cooked chicken
- 40g sliced mini pepperoni
- 40g diced red pepper
- Pinch chilli flakes

Directions:

2. Spread the bbq sauce over each pitta bread.
3. Sprinkle on the cheddar and mozzarella.
4. Top each pitta with the chicken, pepperoni, red pepper and chilli flakes.
5. Cook the pittas one at a time in your air fryer on 180°C for 7 minutes.
6. Repeat until all the pizzas are cooked.
7. Serve with a side salad.

Nutritional Value (Amount per Serving):

Calories: 215; Fat: 12.67; Carb: 9.51; Protein: 15.63

Dynamite Shrimp

Prep Time: 5 Mins
Cook Time: 15 Mins   Serves: 6

Ingredients:

- or The Shrimp (Prawn) Marinade
- 450g Shrimp (Prawns), deveined and shelled
- 1/2 tsp Red Chilli Powder
- 1 tsp Paprika
- 1/2 tsp Salt
- 1 tbsp Soy Sauce
- 1 Egg
- 50g Buttermilk or another Egg
- or The Sauce

- 115g Mayonnaise
- 1 tbsp Sriracha Sauce
- 3 1/2 tbsp Sweet Chilli Sauce
- or The Cornflour Mix
- 75g Cornflour
- 120g Plain Flour
- 1 tsp Garlic Granules
- Other
- 1 tbsp Oil for brushing Prawns

Directions:

1. Combine Prawns with all the ingredients listed under Shrimp (Prawns) in a bowl and set aside.
2. Combine all the ingredients for the sauce in a small bowl and whisk together.
3. Combine all the ingredients for the Cornflour mix in a bowl and whisk together.
4. Preheat air fryer to 200°C.
5. Brush the inside of the air fryer with Oil.
6. Coat the marinaded Prawns in the Cornflour mix in batches.
7. Add to the air fryer leaving space between shrimp.
8. Cover and cook for 5 minutes.
9. After 5 minutes, flip and brush over some oil.
10. Cover and cook for a further 2 – 4 minutes or until cooked.
11. Drizzle sauce over the shrimp and serve immediately.

Nutritional Value (Amount per Serving):

Calories: 339; Fat: 13.44; Carb: 31.01; Protein: 22.33

Smoked Fish Pie With Gnocchi Topping

Prep Time: 10 Mins
Cook Time: 30 Mins   Serves: 4

Ingredients:

- 1 x 180g tub soft cheese
- 100ml vegetable stock,
- made with one stock cube
- 1 tbsp cornflour, mixed with
- 1 tbsp cold water
- 1 x 340g pack fish pie mix,
- salmon, smoked haddock
- and white fish
- 500g shop-bought
- fresh gnocchi
- 2 tbsp vegetable oil
- 75g frozen peas
- 75g frozen sweetcorn
- 5g fresh flat-leaf
- parsley, chopped
- Salt and black pepper

Directions:

1. Place the cream cheese into a bowl, add the stock and cornflour mixture, whisk well until combined. Season with salt and pepper then gently stir in the fish. Transfer to a roasting tin that fits into the air fryer, approximately 22cm x 22cm x 5cm deep.
2. Place the dish onto the air fryer tray and set the fryer temperature to 180°C for 10 minutes.
3. Meanwhile place the gnocchi in a bowl and toss with the oil so that the gnocchi are fully coated in the oil.
4. Remove the fish pie from the air fryer and stir through the peas, sweetcorn and ¾ of the parsley. Place the gnocchi evenly over the fish pie and return to the air fryer set to 190°C for a further 15-20 minutes until the sauce is bubbling and the gnocchi is crisp and golden.
5. Sprinkle with the remaining parsley and serve with some fresh seasonal vegetables.

Nutritional Value (Amount per Serving):

Calories: 701; Fat: 47.43; Carb: 36.29; Protein: 34.58

Spiced Lentil Shepherd'S Pie

Prep Time: 15 Mins
Cook Time: 45 Mins   Serves: 4

Ingredients:

- 1 medium carrot, peeled
- and finely diced
- 1 medium onion, diced
- 1 stick celery, finely diced
- 2 tbsp vegetable oil
- 175g chestnut mushrooms,
- washed and roughly
- chopped
- ½ tsp chilli powder
- 2 tsp ground cumin
- 2 tbsp tomato puree
- 400g can finely
- chopped tomatoes
- Vegetable stock
- 2 x 400g cans of lentils,
- drained and rinsed
- 1 tbsp cornflour, mixed with

- 2 tbsp cold water
- Topping
- 1.2kg sweet potato, peeled
- and diced into 2cm chunks
- 20g vegan spread

Directions:

1. Put the carrot, onion and celery into a 23cm square roasting tin and drizzle over the oil. Put onto the air fryer tray, set the air fryer temperature to 180°C and cook for 8 minutes, until the vegetables have softened. Stir halfway through.
2. Stir in the mushrooms and spices to the roasting tin and mix well. Cook for a further 5 minutes.
3. Add tomato puree, canned tomatoes, stock, lentils and cornflour. Return to the air fryer and continue to cook for 18 minutes.
4. Meanwhile, boil the sweet potatoes for 15-18 minutes, then drain, add butter, and mash until smooth. Season to taste.
5. Spread the mashed sweet potato over the lentil mixture and cook for 15 minutes at 190°C, until the sauce is bubbling and the potatoes are golden.

Nutritional Value (Amount per Serving):

Calories: 936; Fat: 42.63; Carb: 83.02; Protein: 65.55

Chapter 7: Desserts

Sticky Toffee Pudding With Hot Toffee Sauce

Prep Time: 20 Mins
Cook Time: 30 Mins   Serves: 6

Ingredients:

- Traybake
- 115g dried stoned dates,
- roughly chopped
- 50ml boiling water
- 115g butter, plus
- extra for greasing
- 55g golden caster sugar
- 55g soft brown sugar
- 2 medium eggs
- 115g SR flour
- ½ tsp baking powder
- 50g pecan nuts,
- roughly chopped

- Toffee Sauce
- 80g unsalted butter
- 150g soft dark brown sugar
- 150ml single cream

Directions:

1. Place the dates in a small bowl and pour over the boiling water. Leave to stand for about 15 minutes, until the dates absorb the water. Mash with a fork, then leave to cool completely.
2. Grease and line a 20cm x 3cm square cake tin with parchment paper.
3. In a bowl, beat the butter, caster sugar and brown sugar with an electric whisk for 2-3 minutes, until light and fluffy.
4. Add the eggs, dates, flour and baking powder and beat the mixture for 1-2 minutes, until well blended. Gently stir in the pecan nuts.
5. Set the air fryer temperature to 170°C and preheat for 3 minutes. Meanwhile, spoon the cake mixture into the prepared tin and level the top with the back of a spoon.
6. Bake in the preheated air fryer for 25-30 minutes, until well risen, golden brown and firm to the touch. Insert a skewer into the centre of the cake; it should come out clean if cooked.
7. To prepare the toffee sauce, place all of the ingredients into a saucepan, gently bring to the boil then simmer gently for 5 minutes, or until the sauce has thickened.
8. Cut the warm sponge into portions and serve with the hot toffee sauce.

Nutritional Value (Amount per Serving):

Calories: 839; Fat: 43.62; Carb: 78.04; Protein: 37.13

Orange Poppyseed Loaf Cake

Prep Time: 10 Mins
Cook Time: 50 Mins   Serves: 6

Ingredients:

- or The Cake
- 130g Butter
- 130g Caster Sugar
- 2 Eggs
- 130g Self Raising Flour
- 25g Poppyseeds, lightly toasted
- 1 Orange, Zest only
- or The Icing
- 1/2 Juice of Orange
- 150g Icing Sugar, sieved

Directions:

1. Add the Butter and Sugar to a bowl and beat till creamy. Around 5 minutes.
2. Add the Eggs one at a time, beating after each addition until fully incorporated
3. Sieve in the Self Raising Flour and fold in along with the Poppyseeds and Orange Zest.
4. Line a loaf tin with greaseproof paper or a loaf liner or use a rectangular metal takeaway container.
5. Add the Cake batter and level out.
6. Preheat the Air Fryer.
7. Set to 150°C and bake for 40 minutes.
8. Once it is ready, place the loaf tin in the centre and leave to bake.
9. Check that the cake is baked through by inserting a skewer into the middle and ensuring that is comes out clean.
10. Meanwhile mix the Orange Juice and Icing Sugar together in a bowl.
11. Leave the cake in the tin until it is cool before removing.
12. Top with Icing.

Nutritional Value (Amount per Serving):

Calories: 366; Fat: 19.8; Carb: 40.54; Protein: 7.58

Heavenly Melting Moments

Prep Time: 5 Mins
Cook Time: 8 Mins   Serves: 9

Ingredients:

- 100g Butter
- 75g Caster Sugar
- 150g Self Raising Flour
- 1 Small Egg
- 50g White Chocolate
- 3Tbsp Desiccated Coconut
- 1Tsp Vanilla Essence

Directions:

1. Preheat the air fryer to 180°C.
2. Cream the butter and sugar in a large bowl until light and fluffy.
3. Beat in the eggs and then add the vanilla essence.
4. Using a rolling pin bash the white chocolate so that they make a mix of tiny and small pieces.
5. Add the white chocolate and flour and mix well.
6. Roll into small balls and cover in the coconut.
7. Place the balls into the air fryer on cooking tray and cook for eight minutes at 180°C. Reduce the temperature to 160°C for a further 4 minutes so that they can cook in the middle.
8. Serve!

Nutritional Value (Amount per Serving):

Calories: 147; Fat: 6.78; Carb: 18.23; Protein: 2.87

Half Cooked Air Fryer Lemon Biscuits

Prep Time: 5 Mins
Cook Time: 5 Mins   Serves: 9

Ingredients:

- 100g Butter
- 100g Caster Sugar
- 225g Self Raising Flour
- 1 Small Lemon (rind and juice)
- 1 Small Egg
- 1Tsp Vanilla Essence

Directions:

1. Preheat the air fryer to 180°C.
2. Mix flour and sugar in a bowl. Add the butter and rub it in until your mix resembles breadcrumbs. Shake your bowl regularly so that the fat bits come to the top and so that you know what you have left to rub in.
3. Add the lemon rind and juice along with the egg.
4. Combine and knead until you have lovely soft dough.
5. Roll out and cut into medium sized biscuits.
6. Place the biscuits into the air fryer on the cooking tray and cook for five minutes at 180c.
7. Place on a cooling tray and sprinkle with icing sugar.

Nutritional Value (Amount per Serving):

Calories: 164; Fat: 6.81; Carb: 21.64; Protein: 3.62

Air Fryer 10 Minutes Smartie Cookies

Prep Time: 5 Mins
Cook Time: 5 Mins   Serves: 9

Ingredients:

- 100g Butter
- 100g Caster Sugar
- 225g Self Raising Flour
- 1Tsp Vanilla Essence
- 5Tbsp Milk
- 3Tbsp Cocoa
- 1/3 Tube Of Smarties
- 50g White Chocolate

Directions:

1. Preheat the air fryer to 180°C.
2. Mix the cocoa, flour and sugar in a large mixing bowl.
3. Rub in the butter and add the vanilla essence and mix really well.
4. Using a rolling pin smash up your white chocolate so that they are a mix of medium and really small chocolate chips.
5. Add the chocolate and the milk to your cookie mix and mix well.
6. Knead your mixture well until it is nice and soft and add a little more milk if you need to.
7. Roll out your mixture and using a cookie cutter form into nice biscuit shapes.
8. Place the Smarties into the top of the cookies so that they are half in the

cookie and half out in the open.
9. Place the cookies into the air fryer on the cooking tray and cook for ten minutes at 180°C.
10. Serve with warm milk.

Nutritional Value (Amount per Serving):

Calories: 185; Fat: 7.27; Carb: 25.55; Protein: 3.81

Air Fryer Super Simple Shortbread Chocolate Balls

Prep Time: 4 Mins
Cook Time: 13 Mins   Serves: 9

Ingredients:

- 175g Butter
- 75g Caster Sugar
- 250g Plain Flour
- 1Tsp Vanilla Essence
- 9 Chocolate chunks
- 2Tbsp Cocoa

Directions:

1. Preheat your air fryer to 180°C.
2. Mix your flour, sugar and cocoa in a bowl together.
3. Rub in your butter and knead well until you have a smooth dough.
4. Divide into balls and place a chunk of chocolate into the centre of each and make sure none of the chocolate chunk is showing.
5. Place your chocolate shortbread balls onto the cooking tray in your air fryer. Cook them at 180°C for 8 minutes and then a further 5 minutes on 160c so that you can make sure they are cooked in the middle.
6. Serve!

Nutritional Value (Amount per Serving):

Calories: 331; Fat: 11.55; Carb: 51.01; Protein: 5.02

CONCLUSION

We enjoy air fryers in part because of the creative features frequently provided to swiftly and evenly cook items. With dual-drawer air fryers, you can simultaneously prepare two separate foods while the appliance manages the timing to guarantee that everything is done at the same time. Or, for large households, make twice as much food with far less oil.

The Salter dual-drawer air fryer is a good option for anyone looking to upgrade their frying capacity from a single-drawer model at an affordable price because it is on the lower end of the price spectrum. It is also smaller than you may imagine, with dimensions of 40 cm, 36 cm, and 32 cm.

It fits beneath low-hanging kitchen cabinets for countertop storage and is only 10 cm longer than many of the single-drawer variants we are familiar with. This dual-drawer air fryer is an excellent value if you don't mind a little trial and error to get the perfect cook for your favourite foods.

APPENDIX RECIPE INDEX

A

Air Fryer Tilapia Recipe 18
Air Fried Boiled Eggs 18
Air Fryer Chinese Kebabs Rice 23
Air Fryer Brussels Sprout Crisps 27
Air Fryer Sweet Potato Fries 27
Air Fryer Sliced Potatoes 28
Air Fryer Vegetables 29
Air Fryer Roasted Garlic 29
Air Fryer Chicken Wrapped In Bacon 33
Air Fryer Prawn Paste Chicken Wings 34
Air Fryer Grilled Chicken Sticks 34
Air Fryer Chicken Fried Rice 37
Air Fryer Party Meatballs 40
Air Fryer Scallops With Cheese 40
Air Fryer Roast Pork 41
Air Fryer Ground Beef 43
Air Fryer Thai Meatballs 44
Air Fryer Pigs in Blanket 45
Air Fryer Roast Beef 45
Air Fryer Frozen Samosa 48
Air Fryer Frozen Hash Browns 48
Air Fryer Rhubarb Crumble 49
Air Fryer Tortilla Pizza 50
Air Fryer Grilled Ham And Cheese 51
Air Fryer Chimichanga 51
Air Fryer Omelette 52
Air Fryer Egg And Bacon Pie 55
Air Fryer Chicken Kebabs 57
Air Fryer Frozen Chicken Nuggets 58
Air Fryer Prawns 59
Air Fryer Potatoes 60
Air Fryer Pitta Pizza 61
Air Fryer 10 Minutes Smartie Cookies 69
Air Fryer Super Simple Shortbread Chocolate Balls 70

B

Boiled Eggs With Crispy Asparagus And Parma Ham Soldiers 19

C

Crispy Roast Potatoes 30
Crispy Air Fryer Chicken Breast (Healthier And Juicy) 38
Cheese And Spring Onion Quesadilla 53
Courgette Fritters 54

D

Dino Nuggets In Air Fryer 59
Dynamite Shrimp 61

E

Easy Sage Onion Stuffing Balls 54

F

Frozen Bacon In Air Fryer 43
Frozen Meatballs In Air Fryer 46

H

Herby Chicken Thighs 32
Honey Lemon Chicken Stuffed With Zucchini .. 35
Heavenly Melting Moments 68
Half Cooked Air Fryer Lemon Biscuits 68

O

Orange Poppyseed Loaf Cake 67

R

Roasted Chicken Wings 36
Reheat French Fries In Fryer 58

S

Smoked Salmon, Scrambled Egg And Avocado Toast 21
Sourdough Bruschetta 22
Stuffed Chicken Breast Wrapped In Serrano Ham 32
Spicy Drumsticks With Barbecue Marinade 37
Spicy Country Fries 42
Smoked Fish Pie With Gnocchi Topping 62
Spiced Lentil Shepherd'S Pie 63
Sticky Toffee Pudding With Hot Toffee Sauce ... 66

T

Tuna Pasta Melt 20
Two Ingredient Air Fryer Croutons 23
The Ultimate Fried English Breakfast 24
Traditional Welsh Rarebit Air Fryer Style 25

Printed in Great Britain
by Amazon